The Library of
Political Assassinations

The Assassination of
James A. Garfield

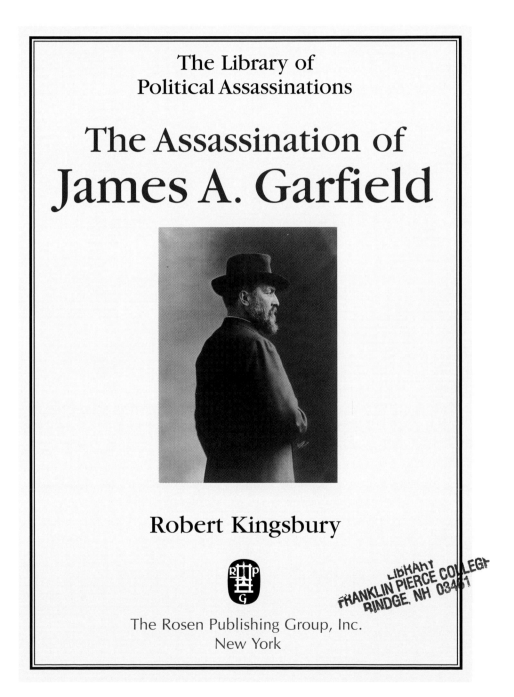

Robert Kingsbury

The Rosen Publishing Group, Inc.
New York

To my mother and father

Published in 2002 by The Rosen Publishing Group, Inc.
29 East 21st Street, New York, NY 10010

First Edition

Library of Congress Cataloging-in-Publication Data

Kingsbury, Robert.
The assassination of James A. Garfield / by Robert Kingsbury. —
1st ed.
p. cm. — (The library of political assassinations)
Includes bibliographical references and index.
Summary: Examines one of America's lesser-known presidents, his assassination, and the life of Charles Guiteau, who killed him.
ISBN 0-8239-3540-X (library binding)
1. Garfield, James A. (James Abram), 1831–1881—Assassination—Juvenile literature. 2. Guiteau, Charles Julius, 1841–1882—Juvenile literature. 3. Assassins—United States—Biography—Juvenile literature. [1. Garfield, James A. (James Abram), 1831–1881—Assassination. 2. Guiteau, Charles Julius, 1841–1882. 3. Assassins.]
I. Title. II. Series.
E687.9 .K56 2002
973.8'4'092—dc21

Manufactured in the United States of America

(Previous page) James Garfield served briefly as president of the United States in 1881. He was shot in July of that year by a disgruntled political candidate and died in September.

Contents

This monument to President Garfield in Cleveland, Ohio, was completed in 1890.

Introduction

Washington, Jefferson, Lincoln, Roosevelt: These are household names to many Americans, the names of presidents whose achievements have long been celebrated by historians. The chances are that you are carrying the likeness of one or more of these men on the coins in your pocket.

This book is about a man whose name is not so well known, and whose face you won't find on a coin. James Abram Garfield (1831–1881) is sometimes remembered as the last of the log-cabin presidents. At other times, he is recalled as the victim of a mad assassin. But he spent too little time in the White House—less than 200 days (nearly half on his deathbed)—to leave much of a stamp on the office or on our national memory.

Garfield was president in an era when elected officials walked freely among the nation's citizens. There was no Secret Service in his day; he had no bodyguards. And Garfield would not have had it any other way. He once said, "Assassination can no more be guarded against than death by lightning; and it is best not to worry about either." This was also a time in history when the president was responsible for making appointments for thousands of government positions.

These two aspects of the presidency in Garfield's day—the close contact with thousands of job applicants and the lack of personal protection—factored significantly in his assassination. Charles Guiteau, the man who murdered Garfield, initially came calling at the White House in the hope of obtaining a diplomatic assignment. It was the lack of adequate security that enabled him to approach and shoot the president.

The fact is that we will never know what kind of a president James Garfield might have become had Charles Guiteau not ended his life at the age of forty-nine. As it is, Garfield's name will surface from time to time in the reports of grade school students and in the rare accounts of scholars and historians. But his name and his face may never be famous in the same way as those of other past presidents.

The twists of destiny that eventually led Garfield and Guiteau to the same spot at the same ill-fated moment provide great drama and great suspense. The unstable Guiteau, at times believing himself an heroic patriot and at times a holy instrument of God, presents a human portrait that is almost too strange to believe. Surely, the bizarre story of President James Garfield's assassination cannot fail to fascinate even the casual reader of history.

The Shooting

The carriage of James Garfield, twentieth president of the United States, and his secretary of state, James Blaine, neared the depot of the Baltimore & Potomac Railroad. Inside the station, a man paced nervously in the ladies' waiting room, anticipating the president's arrival. In his jacket pocket he held a .44-caliber pistol. The man was Charles Guiteau. He had purchased the gun more than three weeks earlier. He had carefully chosen a model with a fancy handle, because he felt it would look good in a museum one day. Guiteau would later say that he had been inspired by God to commit the terrible act he now contemplated on that Saturday morning of July 2, 1881.

Guiteau was desperate to accomplish his mission. Since buying the gun, he had prepared to shoot the president on at least four other occasions, but each time something had prevented him from seeing the crime through. Three weeks earlier, on the morning of Sunday, June 12, Guiteau had stood at the back of a crowded church, his pistol at the ready, hoping to get a clear shot at Garfield as he worshiped.

Because of his poor aim, he feared he would miss the president and hit someone else. Once the church had emptied after the service, Guiteau checked outside to see if he would have a clear shot through one of the windows. The following Wednesday, Guiteau returned to the church to rehearse his plan for Sunday.

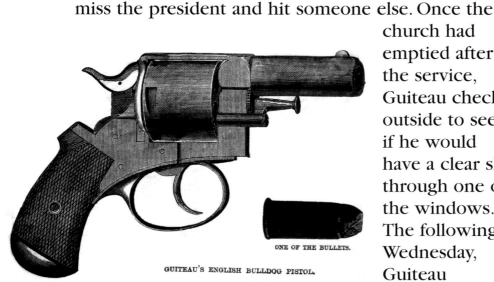

ONE OF THE BULLETS.

GUITEAU'S ENGLISH BULLDOG PISTOL.

Charles Guiteau used this pistol to kill President James Garfield.

A New Plan

Guiteau soon learned that a new plan would have to be devised: President Garfield would not be at the church on Sunday. He was to accompany his wife, Lucretia, on a trip to Long Branch, New Jersey, on Saturday morning. Mrs. Garfield had been sick since late April, and it was thought that the fresh ocean air at Long Branch would do her good. Guiteau decided to try to get to Garfield at the station before the president left Washington, D.C.

On the morning of Saturday, June 18, Guiteau arrived at the depot before the Garfields. He made his way to the waiting room, but his nerve failed him that day. He later wrote of this second failed attempt: "I intended to remove the President this morning at the depot, as he took the cars for Long Branch; but Mrs. Garfield looked so thin, and clung so tenderly to the President's arm, my heart failed me to part them."

President Garfield stayed in Long Branch for a week and a half. It was during this time that Charles Guiteau did a very strange thing. He paid a visit to the District of Columbia jail, where he expected to be taken after his crime was car-

THE JAIL

Guiteau visited the District of Columbia jail, where he expected to be imprisoned after carrying out his crime.

ried out. He was hoping to have a tour of the place. Instead he settled for a peek through the door. All in all, he judged it a most "excellent jail."

The president returned to the capital at the end of June for a few days of work before he was to begin his summer-long vacation on July 2. During the four days before Garfield's departure, Guiteau watched the White House constantly, hoping the opportunity to act would present itself. He had developed the habit of waiting

Entered according to Act of Congress by M.B.Brady & Co. in the year 1865 in the Clerk's Office of the District Court of the District of Columbia.

This is a portrait of Secretary of State James Blaine, who was with Garfield when he was shot. Blaine chased Guiteau briefly before returning to the president's side.

on a bench in Lafayette Park, across from the White House. From there he was able to observe the comings and goings of the president.

On the night of June 29, Guiteau was at his post in Lafayette Park, gun in pocket, waiting for Garfield to return from an evening carriage ride with two of his sons, Hal and Jim. But the long hours of watching and waiting and the heat of summer had tired Guiteau. He gave up and went back to the boarding house where he was staying before the Garfields returned.

Two evenings later, on July 1, Garfield came out of the White House and walked the two blocks to Secretary of State Blaine's house. He was alone. Guiteau followed. Garfield reached Blaine's house safely. Half an hour later, Garfield emerged with Blaine. Guiteau would later remark that the two men were "in the most delightful and cozy fellowship possible; just as hilarious as two young girls." He followed them a short way, but again Guiteau's resolve failed him. He felt "tired and wearied from the heat" and decided to go home.

And so, as he waited anxiously for the president to arrive at the station on that ill-fated Saturday morning, Charles Guiteau was well aware that this represented his last and best chance to accomplish his terrible scheme for some time to come and perhaps forever.

At the Station

President Garfield's carriage arrived at the Baltimore & Potomac Railroad depot. As the president and Blaine

Guiteau shot President Garfield at the Baltimore & Potomac Railroad depot in Washington, D.C.

stepped from the carriage outside the depot, Patrick Kearney, the police officer on duty at the B Street entrance, told the president that it was 9:20 AM. The train would be leaving in ten minutes.

This artist's depiction shows the chaos and confusion at the scene of President Garfield's assassination.

Garfield and Blaine waited outside together for a few moments. Two of the president's five children—Hal, age seventeen, and Jim, age fifteen—were following in a second carriage. The other two Garfield boys—Irvin, age ten, and Abe, age eight—were visiting relatives in Ohio. Mollie, age fourteen, Garfield's only daughter, was with her mother in Long Branch. The president was expecting to meet his wife and daughter later that day.

It was time to board the train. Garfield and Blaine stepped inside the station into the ladies' waiting room. Guiteau was waiting. The two men were about halfway across the room when Guiteau approached from behind and fired his revolver. His first shot grazed the president's right arm. Garfield cried out, "My God! What is this?!" Then there was a second shot. This one struck Garfield on the right side of his lower back. The president fell to the floor.

Blaine's first reaction was to chase Guiteau, who had made for the B Street exit. He then thought better of it and turned back to attend to the president. At the sound of the shots, Officer Kearney rushed into the depot. He ran right into Guiteau as he was hurrying out. Although he didn't know of Guiteau's involvement with the gunfire, Kearney's instincts told him to hold the man until he learned what had happened. Guiteau put up no resistance.

The scene inside the ladies' waiting room was chaos. The president, who was lying on the carpet in a pool of blood, was alive, but badly wounded. Sarah White, the ladies' room attendant, cradled Garfield's head in her lap. Hal and Jim were at their father's side.

Jim was in tears. Hal was doing his best to stay calm. A carriage was sent to fetch a doctor. Then a mattress was taken from one of the rail cars and Garfield was lifted onto it.

Shortly afterward, Dr. D. W. Bliss arrived on the scene. He examined the wound in Garfield's back and tried to find the bullet by inserting his finger into the bullet hole. Garfield, still on the mattress, was carried to the second floor of the depot to a private area.

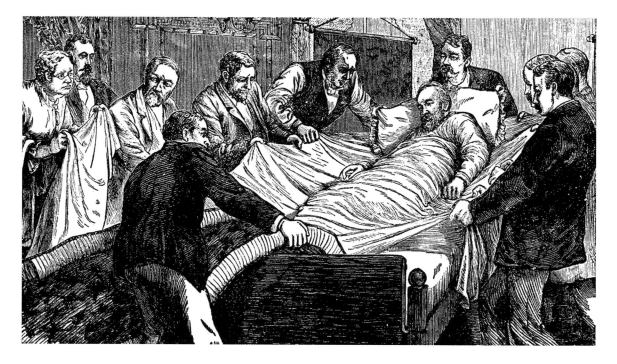

This drawing shows the wounded Garfield being transferred from a mattress to a bed.

Several other doctors were now arriving. One of them said some encouraging words to the president, who replied simply, "Thank you, Doctor, but I am a dead man." It is safe to say that at that moment no one in the room disagreed with him.

Other than poking around in Garfield's wound to look for the bullet, the doctors were clearly at a loss as to what to do for the president. The patient, for his part, was growing impatient, asking repeatedly to be taken to the White House. Finally, at around 10:45 AM, Garfield, still on the mattress, was transported to a carriage and on to the White House.

Police Headquarters

Meanwhile, at the district police headquarters, Guiteau was not arguing his guilt. "I did it and will go to jail for it," he announced. In all the excitement of getting Guiteau out of the rail depot and to the police station, Officer Kearney had not thought until now to search Guiteau for the weapon. The gun was found in his pocket, along with a letter dated that morning and addressed to the White House. Guiteau wrote in the letter that the "President's death was a sad necessity, but it will unite the Republican party and save the Republic." We will see later that Guiteau's motive was much less clear than this patriotic declaration suggests.

Back at the White House, Garfield's doctors did not expect him to survive the night. Not only did he live to see the sun rise the next day, but he lived to see many more sunrises. But the fallen president would never again leave his bed under his own power.

Coming of Age

In July 1881, citizens across the thirty-eight United States were asking, Who is this Charles Guiteau? And why did he shoot our president? Today's readers, unfamiliar with this period in our nation's history, may also be wondering: Who for that matter, was James Garfield?

Who, indeed. Who were these two men, the lead players in the American tragedy of the summer of 1881? A brief glance back at the life of each man is perhaps the best place to begin for those who seek an answer to this question.

When Charles Guiteau was born in Freeport, Illinois, in 1841, James Garfield was two months shy of his tenth birthday and living in a log cabin in northeastern Ohio. Young James, whose father died before he had reached the age of two, was a big, strapping boy who was frequently confined to bed during his childhood due to both injury and illness. James was the youngest of five Garfield children.

Destined for Greatness

From James's earliest days, his mother, Eliza, assured him that he was destined for greatness. Although she sent her four oldest children to school, in James's case, education became so important that Mrs. Garfield offered a corner of her land for the construction of a small schoolhouse. A teacher was brought in so James and his siblings would no longer have to walk the six-mile round trip to school each day.

By the time he had reached his teens, James was working on nearby farms to help his mother make ends meet. At sixteen, he yearned for a life at sea. He traveled to the nearest port, which was Cleveland on Lake Erie, to sign on as a sailor, but was frightened away from the first ship he visited by a surly, drunken captain. Closer to home, a relative found James a position on a canal boat. This was not the high seas (or even Lake Erie), but for the young Garfield, it was a great adventure.

On returning home, James spoke excitedly about his six weeks on the canals. He had fallen off the boat and nearly drowned no fewer than fourteen times! His mother began to fear that James would choose a career on the canals that did not come close to meeting the standards she had set for her son.

C.&O. CANAL

The young Garfield wanted to live and work on canal boats like this one.

17

She convinced him to enroll at Geauga Seminary. To her great relief, he adored his teachers, his classmates, and his studies, and he soon abandoned his dream of a life on the canals. To pay for his room, board, clothing, and school supplies at Geauga, James worked odd jobs in the community. Later, he taught classes. After a year and a half at the school, James left to attend the Western Reserve Eclectic Institute.

A Rocky Start

While James was thriving in school, Charles Guiteau was experiencing a much more difficult life in Freeport,

GUITEAU'S FATHER.

Luther Guiteau, a cold, stern man, raised Charles and his siblings after their mother died.

Illinois. His mother, who had never truly recovered from Charles's birth, lost two babies during Charles's first years. She died when he has seven, leaving young Charles in the hands of his cold, stern father, Luther. Charles had an older brother and sister. His brother, John, thought him spoiled and difficult. He was never very close to Charles. But Frances, his sister, held Charles in great affection. She raised her little brother until his early teens. Then she married and moved to Chicago.

Not a lot is known about Guiteau's childhood. According to letters, family papers, the accounts of people who knew him, and the man's own statements, Charles was lonely and isolated as a child. He appears to have had few if any friends. He was hyperactive and fidgety. Charles's father once offered him a dime if he could sit still for five minutes. He couldn't. There was also a history of mental illness in the Guiteau family bloodline. Charles's later behavior suggests that he may have inherited this illness.

A Study in Contrasts

Where the young James Garfield reveled in hard work and the praise it brought him, Charles Guiteau did not. At sixteen, he left home and found work in Davenport, Iowa, but was fired after a very short time on the job. When Charles's grandfather died in 1859, he inherited $1,000—a great sum of money in those days.

Charles's grandfather had believed that of all his grandchildren, only Charles had talent. He thought that with help, the young man might make something of himself. Charles had hoped to attend the University of Michigan at Ann Arbor. However, after failing the entrance examination, Charles learned that he would have to go to preparatory school to bring his level up. But Guiteau never gave himself a chance in his studies. Before long, he had quit the prep school and abandoned his plans for a university degree.

Religious Beliefs

Both Garfield and Guiteau were raised by parents who were members of small Christian sects. Luther Guiteau, Charles's father, admired John Humphrey Noyes. Noyes believed that it was possible for people to become perfect and that he himself had already attained perfection. Many Christians thought the idea was not in line with traditional Christian beliefs.

Noyes founded the Oneida Community in an isolated area of New York State in 1848. There, community members lived off the fruits of their labors and strove to attain the perfection promised by their leader.

As Charles neared his twentieth birthday, aimless and unemployed, Luther Guiteau advised his son to go to Oneida and join Noyes's community. Luther believed the members' high ideals and commitment to hard work would dampen the flights of imagination that led his son to think he would one day be ruler of the world.

Die Oneida Community in Lenor, New-York. — Die Genossenschaft beim Mittagsmahl.

Charles Guiteau was apparently not very happy with the hard work and communal living of the Oneida Community.

Charles agreed to give it a try, and in 1861 he moved to Oneida. He remained there some four years, but throughout his stay, he had difficulty fitting in. He did not enjoy the hard work. He got along poorly with the other members, and he disliked the community's policy of openly criticizing members as a way to help them achieve perfection. At least one historian has suggested that Guiteau may have stayed on at Oneida to avoid fighting in the Civil War (1861–1865).

For his part, James Garfield was a devoted member of the Disciples of Christ from a very young age. The Disciples called for a return to worship focused entirely on basic Christian beliefs, which holds that Jesus Christ is the savior of humankind and that the Bible is the only source of God's truth.

During his time at the Eclectic Institute, it seemed quite possible that young Garfield would become a preacher. It was not unusual to find him addressing a Sunday gathering of the Disciples from the time he turned twenty until he entered politics at the age of twenty-eight. Even at twenty, James was considered a gifted orator, or speaker, greatly admired for his eloquence and passionate delivery.

Not only was Garfield a good student at the Eclectic Institute, but he quickly became a respected teacher. One of his classmates (and later his student) was Lucretia Rudolph. She was a quiet, timid girl who would, some seven years later, become Mrs. Lucretia Garfield.

James A. Garfield Timeline

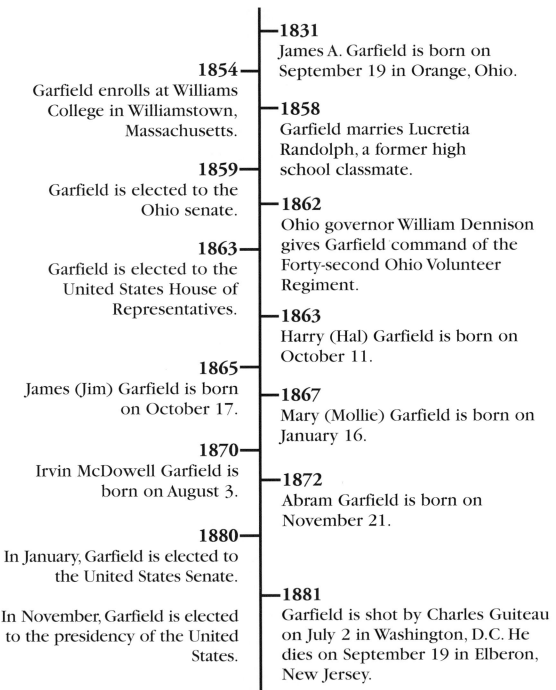

1831
James A. Garfield is born on September 19 in Orange, Ohio.

1854
Garfield enrolls at Williams College in Williamstown, Massachusetts.

1858
Garfield marries Lucretia Randolph, a former high school classmate.

1859
Garfield is elected to the Ohio senate.

1862
Ohio governor William Dennison gives Garfield command of the Forty-second Ohio Volunteer Regiment.

1863
Garfield is elected to the United States House of Representatives.

1863
Harry (Hal) Garfield is born on October 11.

1865
James (Jim) Garfield is born on October 17.

1867
Mary (Mollie) Garfield is born on January 16.

1870
Irvin McDowell Garfield is born on August 3.

1872
Abram Garfield is born on November 21.

1880
In January, Garfield is elected to the United States Senate.

In November, Garfield is elected to the presidency of the United States.

1881
Garfield is shot by Charles Guiteau on July 2 in Washington, D.C. He dies on September 19 in Elberon, New Jersey.

In the fall of 1854, just shy of his twenty-third birthday, Garfield enrolled at Williams College in Williamstown, Massachusetts. Having spent virtually his entire life to up that point in just a few counties of rural northeastern Ohio, Garfield's experience in the East was a great revelation to him. To his eastern-born class-mates, Garfield must have seemed like a country boy from the untamed "West." Nevertheless, it was not long before Garfield established himself at Williams as a gifted student, a fine public speaker, and a trusted friend.

A Rising Star

In the five years that separated Garfield's graduation from Williams College and the start of the Civil War in 1861, Garfield returned to Ohio, to his family, his friends, and the Eclectic Institute. He taught classes in Latin, Greek, mathematics, history, philosophy, English litera-ture, grammar, and geology for a year before becoming head of the school. Garfield continued to preach on Sundays. He was often asked to appear at speaking events covering scientific, literary, and, of course, reli-gious topics. He began to appear at political rallies and was considered one of Ohio's budding orators.

In 1858 Garfield's name surfaced as a possible Republican candidate for the Ohio senate. Eager to have an impact on a larger stage, Garfield did nothing to discourage the talk. Before long, his name began to appear on petitions and, finally, on the ballot. Garfield gave some thirty campaign speeches before the election, most of them focused on the question of limiting slavery. He was a Republican candidate running in a Republican district. He won easily, and in January 1860, at the age of twenty-eight, he took up his seat in the Ohio senate.

That year there was a presidential election. The Republican nominee was Abraham Lincoln. James Garfield made more than fifty speeches in support of Lincoln. He spoke to people from all walks of life and his reputation as a public speaker grew throughout the state of Ohio.

The Civil War

The country was moving quickly toward civil war. When war broke out on April 12, 1861, Garfield was well positioned within Ohio's government over the issues of slavery and states' rights. He received an important military position. As a history buff, Garfield knew that a successful career as a military leader could help pave the way for a political career.

Perhaps this was his chief motivation, in the spring of 1861, for wanting to command a regiment. Who can say for certain? We know that Garfield was an ambitious man, but we also know that he was passionately patriotic. He was increasingly convinced that not only should the spread of slavery be stopped, but that it should be abolished altogether.

In late summer 1861, Garfield's friend, Ohio governor William Dennison, named him colonel of the Forty-second Ohio Volunteer Regiment. It was Garfield's job to recruit and train his men. He found most of the volunteers he needed among the students, faculty, and graduates of the Eclectic Institute. Garfield's role in the Civil War was minor, and yet he handled his responsibilities well. He was eventually promoted to major general. President Lincoln granted the promotion himself, after Garfield made a daring ride on horseback across battle lines to deliver a message to a Union general. He wanted to alert the general of the position of the Confederate forces. To do this, he had to cross the line of fire.

In 1863, Garfield was elected to the House of Representatives. He resigned his military commission and took his seat in Congress when President Lincoln insisted that he would serve

Garfield, photographed in his uniform, had a successful military career and was promoted to the rank of major general.

his country better in Washington than on the battlefield. Garfield represented his Ohio district for the next nineteen years. He would, in time, become one of the most powerful Republicans of his day.

CHAS. J. GUITEAU,

ASSASSIN OF THE PRESIDENT.

Entered according to act of Congress, in the year 1881, by
C. M. BELL,
in the office of the Librarian of Congress, at Washington, D. C.

Charles J. Guiteau. ("Chas" is a commonly used abbreviation of Charles.)

Guiteau's World

Sadly, Charles Guiteau did not fare as well as Garfield in his career. Toward the end of the war, Guiteau left the Oneida Community and traveled to New York City with the intention of founding a religious newspaper. He was unsuccessful in obtaining money to support the project and soon dropped the idea.

Guiteau then hit upon the notion of suing Noyes for unpaid wages for the many years he had worked at Oneida. It mattered little to him that he had signed a contract agreeing to receive room and board in exchange for his work. He hoped to recover more than $9,000 in lost wages. He also threatened to launch a negative publicity campaign exposing the way the community handled relations between men and women. At Oneida, monogamous relationships were discouraged. Community members were regularly assigned "husbands" and "wives" by the group's leaders.

But Guiteau had lied about himself, a practice that became quite common for him in the years to come. He falsely claimed that he had connections to two New York newspapers, and Noyes moved to expose him. In a desperate effort to not walk away empty-handed, Guiteau lowered his demand to $1,000 before dropping his claim altogether.

For the next fourteen years, Guiteau tried his hand at a number of professions. He was, at different times, a lawyer, a debt collector, an insurance agent, a journalist, an evangelist, and a political speaker. At least, that is how he described himself on his business cards. Perhaps because of his dislike for hard work, or perhaps because of his difficult nature, Guiteau never made much of any of his jobs.

The one line of work that he was well qualified for was that of debt collector. Because he spent a good deal of time avoiding paying his own debts, he knew all the tricks. In fact, he was very effective at collecting debts, but had a nasty habit of pocketing the money he collected instead of returning it to those who had hired him.

Guiteau traveled back and forth from New York to Chicago, avoiding debts, fleeing bill collectors, and seeking fortune. During one of his stints in Chicago, he married Annie Bunn, a librarian at the Young Men's Christian Association (YMCA), who was sixteen, ten years younger than Guiteau. Guiteau treated her miserably during their five years of marriage. More than once, when he was angry with her, he locked her in a closet overnight. Eventually, after much suffering at her husband's hands, Annie Guiteau filed for divorce.

A Downward Spiral

In 1874, Guiteau spent five weeks in the New York City jail for fraud. He was released on bail into the custody of his brother-in-law, George Scoville, husband of his sister, Frances. Charles lived with the Scovilles for a short time in Wisconsin, but the arrangement did not last long. At one point, Charles threatened his sister with an ax.

A doctor called in by Frances found Guiteau unstable and suggested she have him committed to an asylum. But Guiteau slipped away to Chicago before anything could be done about it.

It was around this time that Guiteau wrote *The Truth and the Removal*. He had created the book by copying portions of John Noyes's book, *The Berean*. Guiteau ordered a printing of 1,000 copies. He managed to get 600 from the printer before payment was demanded. Needless to say, he never paid the bill.

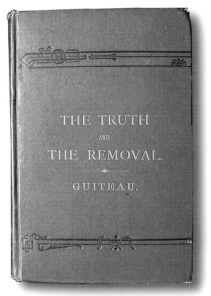

Guiteau copied parts of John Noyes's book *The Berean* in his own book, *The Truth and the Removal*.

Guiteau toured to promote his book; he dreamt of becoming a great evangelist. After three years of crisscrossing the northern and western states of America, Guiteau abandoned his career in religion, remarking that "there is no money in theology." As the 1880 presidential election approached, Guiteau, who had been interested in a political life off and on over the years, decided to try his hand at politics once again. This was an unfortunate decision—both for Charles Guiteau and for his future victim, James Garfield.

President Garfield

Garfield and Guiteau. The names will forever be linked in history. But how is it that two men who had set such different courses for their lives should find their names set down side by side in our nation's record? It was in June 1880, at the Republican National Convention in Chicago, that the paths of both men took a fateful turn and began to gradually converge.

As the convention opened on June 2, there were three men competing for the Republican nomination as their party's candidate for president: John Sherman, the current secretary of the treasury; James Blaine, a senator from Maine; and Ulysses S. Grant, who had already served two terms as president from 1869 to 1877. All three had delegates or supporters at the convention who were ready to vote for their candidate.

As the balloting began, it was clear that the deeply divided Republican Party would not reach an agreement on which of the three candidates would be their nominee. As the ballots were tallied, Grant received more than 300 votes, but he remained far shy of the 378 he needed to secure the nomination. The delegates

This engraving depicts the building where the 1880 Republican National Convention was held in Chicago, Illinois.

of Blaine and Sherman held firm in support of their candidates, but neither man had enough votes to overcome Grant. Garfield, who had come to Chicago in support of Sherman, his fellow Ohioan, received a surprising, single vote on the third ballot. In all likelihood, Garfield was amused by this modest show of support.

An Unlikely Nominee

The lone delegate in support of Garfield held on for his candidate through thirty-three ballots. Then, on the thirty-fourth ballot, Garfield received sixteen votes. And on the next, fifty. On the thirty-sixth ballot, the exhausted delegates, sensing a shift in the tide, threw their support behind Garfield, giving him 399 votes. He had won his party's nomination. James A. Garfield became the Republican candidate in the 1880 presidential election.

It is safe to say that these developments stunned Garfield. Although his name had come up in discussions of the presidential candidates earlier that spring, Garfield had never taken the matter very seriously. He had only just been elected to his first term in the U. S. Senate that January, and looked forward to the new challenge. As far as he was concerned, he was not a candidate. But his party thought otherwise.

This campaign medal supporting the presidency of James A. Garfield praises him as a "Soldier, Statesman, President."

Grant's supporters, who called themselves Stalwarts, were not at all pleased with the way things had worked out. In an effort to hold the party together, Chester Alan Arthur, a Grant supporter from New York, was nominated to be Garfield's running mate. Many Stalwarts, chief among them Roscoe Conkling, a senator from New York, remained very unhappy with the Garfield nomination. The rift between Garfield and Conkling would widen in the months ahead and further divide the Republican Party.

Guiteau and the Republicans

Republican Party headquarters were located at the Fifth Avenue Hotel in New York City that summer. It was there that the party leaders gathered to discuss ways to win the presidential election in November. And it was there that Charles Guiteau, eager to demonstrate his commitment to the Republican Party and to James Garfield, began to make regular appearances.

Curiously, only months before, Guiteau had drafted a speech in support of Ulysses Grant. When he learned that Garfield had received the nomination and not Grant, Guiteau quickly reworked parts of the speech to reflect his support of Garfield.

Guiteau had many copies of the speech printed. It became his calling card. As he greeted party members at the hotel, he pressed copies of the speech into their hands and expressed his eagerness to deliver it on Garfield's behalf.

There is no question that Guiteau met many party leaders that summer, Blaine and Arthur among them. Guiteau believed that he was gaining acceptance among these important men. In truth, the only impression he made on them—if any—was that of a strange character and a nuisance. Determined though he was to deliver his speech, Guiteau managed only once to gather a small audience to hear him.

The more Guiteau mingled among the Republicans at party headquarters, the more he convinced himself that he was playing a key role in Garfield's presidential campaign. He also believed that in thanks for his support, Garfield would appoint him to a government position if elected president. Guiteau began to entertain hopes of a diplomatic assignment in either Vienna, Austria, or Paris, France. He had no reason—and certainly no qualifications—to justify such hopes.

Garfield's inauguration in Washington, D.C., on March 4, 1881

Garfield Wins the Election

Garfield carried the 1880 presidential election by a narrow margin. After the election in November, Guiteau wasted no time in expressing his interest in a diplomatic post. He wrote to the new president congratulating him on his election and added: "Next spring I expect to marry the daughter of a millionaire and I think we can represent the United States with dignity and grace." The woman to whom he was referring was someone he had seen only once, in church.

Garfield was elected in an era when the president was responsible for making hundreds of civil service appointments. Often referred to as the "spoils system," this meant that the president would show his appreciation for the support of loyal followers by rewarding them (or their friends and family) with positions in the federal government. Garfield soon found himself overwhelmed by the many office seekers who crowded the White House after his inauguration in March. In this respect, Guiteau was not unusual; he was merely one man among thousands claiming his reward.

The difference in Guiteau's case was that he mistakenly believed himself well known and respected in the inner circles of the Republican Party, and by both the president and his recently named secretary of state, James Blaine. Within days of the inauguration, Guiteau had left New York and taken up residence in Washington, D.C. While Garfield complained about the time he wasted listening to the petitions of office seekers, Guiteau stepped up his efforts to secure a diplomatic position. By this time he was writing Garfield and Blaine almost daily, insisting to each that he was close to the other and had been promised an appointment. But for the most part, Guiteau's letters went undelivered, stored by staff workers in the office file cabinets of both men.

A Constant Visitor

Between early March and early May, Guiteau was a regular visitor at both the White House and the State Department. He was able to see Blaine on a few occasions, but only once did he meet with Garfield, and then only briefly. In his letters to Garfield, Guiteau frequently made reference to the speech he had written during the presidential campaign. Guiteau claimed that his speech had a great influence on the course of the election. Somehow, Guiteau gained admission to a White House reception on April 30, at which he met Mrs. Garfield. He made a point of letting her know how important he had been in her husband's election.

Around this time, Guiteau managed to corner Blaine near the State Department offices. Frustrated by Guiteau's ridiculous demands for a position, Blaine snapped at him, "Never speak to me

A MODEL OFFICE-SEEKER.
"I am a Lawyer, a Theologian and a Politician!"—*Charles J. Guiteau.*

This 1881 political cartoon depicts Charles Guiteau carrying a gun and a demand for President Garfield.

again on the Paris consulship as long as you live!" A few days later, Guiteau wrote a letter to Garfield. In it Guiteau claimed that Blaine was positioning himself to run against him in the next presidential election.

Guiteau was upset by his failure to win a diplomatic post and angry with Blaine for treating him so harshly. He was also troubled by a rift that was weakening the Republican Party. He believed that it threatened the stability of the United States. Two days after writing his letter to Garfield regarding Blaine, Guiteau had an inspiration: "If the president was out of the way, everything would go better." Gradually, this inspiration became, in Guiteau's mind, the solution to the party's problems, and the surest way to smooth his path to success.

By mid-May 1881, the president had filled most of the government positions for which he was responsible. He could now, at long last, turn his attention to matters more vital to the governing of the United States. Guiteau would see to it that Garfield would never have the chance.

A Slow Death

On the evening of July 2, Dr. D. W. Bliss, the Washington physician who had taken charge of Garfield's case, announced to the White House press, "There is no hope for President Garfield. He will probably not live three hours and may die in half an hour. The bullet has pierced the liver and it is a fatal wound." Garfield survived the night. His liver had not been touched. Bliss's statement was merely the beginning of eleven weeks of questionable announcements, diagnoses, and decisions on the part of the president's medical team.

The Medical Team

The team consisted of six doctors, nearly all appointed by Bliss. The two members of the team that Bliss did not appoint were Garfield's cousin Silas Boynton, a homeopathic physician, and Susan Edson, Mrs. Garfield's personal doctor. Bliss forced both doctors into nursing roles. Bliss dismissed Garfield's own personal physician, J. H. Baxter, the night of July 2, and never permitted him to consult on the case.

Nearly a month after the president's death, Boynton prepared a statement in which he claimed that on or around August 8, Garfield had told him that he "had no knowledge of ever having placed himself under the professional care of D. W. Bliss and he did not believe that Dr. Bliss had ever spoken one word to him upon the subject." As it turns out, Mrs. Garfield was not consulted either.

At the time of the assassination, a small but growing number of physicians in Europe and the United States practiced what was known as antiseptic medicine. This meant quite simply that they used sterile instruments, maintained the cleanest, most germ-free conditions possible, and did everything in their powers to keep patients free from infections. Unfortunately for Garfield, Bliss and his team did not practice this approach.

Dr. D. W. Bliss took it upon himself to manage the president's care without consulting either Garfield or his wife.

Shortly after the shooting, countless doctors began to probe the president's wound with their unwashed fingers and unsterilized instruments in search of the bullet. The autopsy of the president's body would later reveal that the bullet had not damaged any major organs as it passed into Garfield's body. It had finally lodged just below the pancreas in an area where it would, in all likelihood, do no further harm. The autopsy would also reveal that the doctors had been grossly mistaken about the path the bullet had taken.

Outside the White House, great crowds gathered during the first days of July, anxiously awaiting news of the president. Medical bulletins written by the Bliss team were posted on large boards. The bulletins provided updates on Garfield's pulse rate, temperature, rate of respiration, and details on his intake of food and liquids. What the public didn't know was that the bulletins were carefully crafted statements that never touched on the more serious aspects of Garfield's condition.

In Search of the Bullet

In the second half of July, Alexander Graham Bell was called in to consult on the case. Bell had recently been experimenting with an instrument that was designed to detect metal in the human body. After conducting a series of tests on other patients with his "induction balance," as he called it, the doctors asked him to bring his equipment into the president's room at the White House to try to locate the bullet.

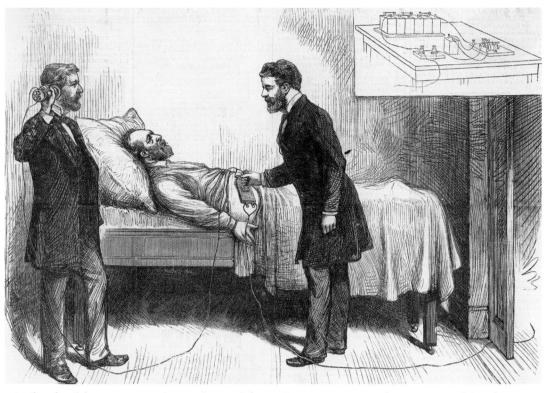

As he had been experimenting with an instrument to detect metal in the human body, Alexander Graham Bell was asked to try to find the bullet in the president's body. The attempt was unsuccessful.

Bell was not successful, but this was not the fault of the machine. The doctors, mistaken about the path of the bullet, had directed Bell to look in an area quite apart from where it actually lay. It is not at all clear what the doctors would have done had the bullet been detected. At no time were they prepared to operate to remove it.

By late August, the once hearty, 210-pound Garfield weighed a mere 130 pounds. And yet to read the headlines of the newspapers, whose writers based their reports on the official bulletins, the patient was "MAKING STEPS TOWARD RECOVERY" and "STEPPING BEYOND DANGER." This could not have been further from the truth. By that time, a steady stream of pus was discharging from Garfield's ears, nose, and mouth, as well as from several incisions the doctors had made. The prospects for the patient's recovery could not have been worse.

VOL. XXX . . . . NO 9324.

A CONSTANT IMPROVEMENT

THE PRESIDENT MUCH BETTER AND MAKING GOOD PROGRESS.

HIS SURGEONS CONFIDENT AND PERFECTLY SATISFIED WITH HIS CONDITION-QUITE AS WELL AS BEFORE THE RELAPSE NO FURTHER SURGICAL OPERATION CONTEMPLATED-A VAST NUMBER OF SENSATIONAL STORIES DENIED.

Washington, July 26.- When Dr. Agnew went into the sickroom this morning the President said to him: "Doctor, I feel much better to-day." The Doctor replied, "You are better, much better, than when I saw you the other day." After the examination Dr. Agnew assured Mrs. Garfield that the condition of the President was as favorable as could be expected and quite encouraging.

This is one example of the official public notices about President Garfield's medical condition that were published in newspapers throughout the nation. Many of these bulletins hid the truth about the severity of Garfield's condition.

At various times during the course of Garfield's ordeal, the press called into question the truth of the official bulletins. Interviews with doctors not connected with the case revealed wide-ranging opinions on Bliss's handling of the president's case. There were accusations of malpractice, but there was also praise for Bliss and his team. Some in the press accused Bliss of manipulating the bulletins in order to benefit in the financial markets. Proof of this, however, was never demonstrated.

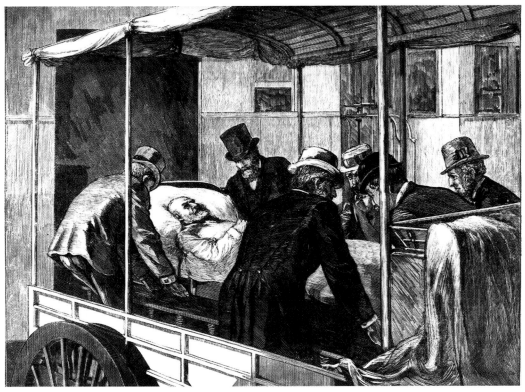

Because his injuries left President Garfield frail, he had to be moved by several men from a wagon to the rail car for a journey to the beach town of Elberon, New Jersey.

To the Beach

The heat and humidity of Washington, D.C., had become too much for Garfield in the first days of September. He insisted on being moved away from the capital. Preparations were made to transport him to the seaside town of Elberon, New Jersey. Because of Garfield's injuries, transporting him necessitated the laying of 3,200 feet of railroad track so that the president could be moved from his rail car directly into the house where he would be staying. On September 6, Garfield made the seven-hour journey from Washington, D.C., to Elberon. Thousands of people lined the route. There was no cheering; there were no smiles. The onlookers stared grimly at the passing train, hats in hand out of respect for their fallen leader.

Although the ocean air and the view of the waves undoubtedly provided Garfield a much-needed mental boost, the change of scenery brought no improvement to his physical condition. He was now in a rapid decline. Incredibly, Bliss and his team were still offering the public hope of a recovery. *The New*

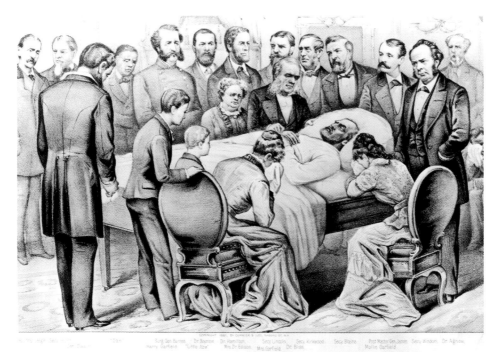

DEATH OF GENERAL JAMES A. GARFIELD,
TWENTIETH PRESIDENT OF THE UNITED STATES.

The president's advisers surround him at his deathbed.

York Times headline of September 10 read "THE PRESIDENT'S BEST DAY." It is small wonder that the nation found itself in a state of shock, when, on September 19 at 10:35 PM, Garfield breathed his last breath. Less than four hours later, before a New York Supreme Court justice, Chester Alan Arthur, Garfield's vice president, took the oath of office as the new president of the United States.

NEWSPAPER

No. 1,358.—Vol. LIII.   NEW YORK, OCTOBER 8, 1881.   [Price, with Supplement, 10 Cents.

THE DEATH OF PRESIDENT GARFIELD.—JUDGE BRADY ADMINISTERING THE PRESIDENTIAL OATH TO VICE-PRESIDENT ARTHUR, AT HIS RESIDENCE IN NEW YORK, SEPTEMBER 20TH.—SEE PAGE 85.

This wood engraving illustrates Chief Justice Brady administering the presidential oath of office to Vice President Chester A. Authur in New York City on September 20, 1881.

The Autopsy

Dr. Bliss and his colleagues supervised Garfield's autopsy. They were joined by a local doctor and a physician from the Army Medical Museum. Bliss later received a good deal of criticism for not allowing a separate team of physicians to supervise the

This artist's representation depicts Garfield's funeral procession at Lakeview Cemetery in Ohio. The ribbon reads "Lay him to sleep whom ye have learned to trust." The top of the arch reads "Come home to rest."

examination. The doctors reported that the cause of death was internal bleeding brought on by a small tear in the splenic artery. The tear was attributed to the bullet. The doctors suggested that an aneurysm had formed around the tear, and had, on the night of Garfield's death, finally given way. There was no mention of the blood poisoning that must surely have been a factor in Garfield's death, judging from the increasing number of infections that had plagued him during his last weeks.

Garfield's body was transported by train to Washington, D.C. He lay in state at the Capitol for nearly a week. During that time, thousands of visitors walked past his coffin to pay their respects. Afterward, Garfield's body was placed on a train for the final journey back to his native Ohio, where he was buried.

Trial and Hanging

Throughout the summer of 1881, while President Garfield's life hung in the balance, Charles Guiteau waited patiently for the rewards that he was sure his act of patriotism would bring. As before the shooting, he believed himself on the path to fame and fortune. Garfield's death that September signaled to Guiteau the next phase in his rise to greatness.

The indictment for the murder of James Garfield was handed down on October 14, 1881. Guiteau responded with a plea of not guilty, which he wrote himself. In it, he articulated three proofs of his innocence: (1) "Insanity, in that it was God's act, not mine." (2) "The president died from malpractice." Three weeks after the shooting, Garfield's doctors announced that he would recover. Two months after that, he died. "Therefore," Guiteau reasoned, "he was not fatally shot." He had simply not received effective medical care. (3) "The president died in New Jersey and, therefore, beyond the jurisdiction of this Court."

This third argument had already been considered by greater legal minds than Guiteau. It had been determined that this would not pose a serious obstacle to the prosecution. But in his first two claims, Guiteau had hit upon the very defense strategies that his own lawyers would choose to pursue.

By today's standards, Guiteau was clearly insane. However, in the nineteenth century, it was believed that the mentally ill caused their illnesses through immoral behavior. There was little sympathy for the president's assassin.

The Best Show in Town

Two lawyers made up the defense team. The first, George Scoville, was Guiteau's brother-in-law from Wisconsin. Leigh Robinson, acting as co-counsel, was appointed by the court when Scoville requested assistance with the case. For his part, Scoville had come to his brother-in-law's aid because he believed him to be mentally ill. He planned to pursue insanity as Guiteau's line of defense. Robinson took the malpractice tack.

From the start, Robinson and Scoville did not get along. As a result, they never managed to coordinate their efforts in the case. To complicate matters further, a third individual insisted that he was the most qualified to argue the defense against the charges: Guiteau himself.

The trial lasted three months. It was the best show in town that winter. Spectators who could not find seats in the courtroom stood. Those who could find seats brought lunches in picnic baskets so as not to lose their seats during the midday recess.

Guiteau did not disappoint. He interrupted anyone and everyone, including Judge Walter Cox. On several occasions, Cox threatened to have Guiteau removed from the courtroom, but despite his assurances that he would behave, Guiteau was never able to restrain himself for long. He ridiculed the prosecutors, he insulted his own lawyers, and he even went so far as to mimic the judge at one point.

On November 19, as the defendant was returning by carriage to the jail after a day at the courthouse, a drunken rider on horseback took a shot at him. Though the bullet pierced his coat, it did not harm him in the least. Nonetheless, for several days afterward, Guiteau avoided standing in the courtroom when he spoke for fear of becoming an easy target.

Toward the end of November, Guiteau took the witness stand. His testimony lasted nearly a week. He recounted his life story and made frequent appeals to the public for money that would, he said, help pay his legal fees. He returned many times to the subject of his innocence. He reminded the court that he had served as God's instrument, that he had been insane on the morning of July 2, and that, in the end, it was the doctors who killed Garfield.

Although Guiteau had a history of erratic behavior and believed that God had directed him to assassinate President Garfield, he was not found insane. Instead, he was sentenced to die.

Following his client's testimony, Scoville resumed his efforts to prove Guiteau's insanity. He called in several expert witnesses, all of whom testified that, based on the facts of the case, the defendant appeared to be insane. In the late nineteenth century, however, the insanity plea was not usually an effective line of defense. It was widely thought that in all but rare instances the insane were responsible for causing their illness through bad and immoral behavior. For this reason, there was very little sympathy for them. Unfortunately, Guiteau had a rather impressive record of criminal, selfish, and immoral acts. This, coupled with the fact that his brother John refused to publicly acknowledge the history of mental illness in the Guiteau family, doomed the Scoville defense from the outset.

Closing arguments for the case ended on January 26, 1882, in the late afternoon. The jury deliberated less than an hour and returned a guilty verdict. The next day Judge Cox issued his sentence: Guiteau would hang on June 30, 1882.

Guiteau's Final Months

Guiteau was unfazed. Even at this late date, he was still convinced that President Arthur or another of the Republican leaders would come to his rescue. After all, he told himself, hadn't he saved the party? He spent a good portion of that spring trying to

THE GALLOWS

EXECUTION OF GUITEAU.—IN THE HANGMAN'S CELL. PULLING THE CORD.

Guiteau pleaded to President Chester A. Arthur for clemency or a pardon, but his appeals for mercy were denied. He was hanged on June 30, 1882, for killing President James Garfield.

profit from his newfound fame. He attempted to sell the suit he wore during the trial for $100, autographs for twenty-five cents, and autographed photos of himself for a dollar.

As his execution day neared, Guiteau began to worry that he would not be released. He sent a letter to Arthur on June 19, 1882, requesting a full pardon. He made a point of reminding the president that it was he who had put him in the executive office. More than 150 doctors who were convinced of Guiteau's insanity also wrote to Arthur, asking that he be spared the death penalty. But there would be neither pardon nor clemency. And so, Guiteau prepared himself for the gallows.

Wanting to make a final, dramatic impression on the public, Guiteau first considered wearing a white robe to his execution. He then decided that wearing only his underwear would be more fitting. The prison chaplain, who spent a great deal of time with him during his last days, eventually talked him out of it. Moments before his hanging, Guiteau read a poem that he had written that morning. He said the idea was "that of a child babbling to his mama and his papa." The refrain of the poem went:

I am going to the Lordy, I am so glad.
I am going to the Lordy, I am so glad.
I am going to the Lordy.
Glory hallelujah! Glory hallelujah!
I am going to the Lordy!

Thus ended the life of Charles Julius Guiteau, assassin of James Abram Garfield, twentieth president of the United States. These two men share a strange chapter in American history. Garfield, who had so hoped to be cherished for his achievements, is instead most remembered for the unusual nature of his untimely death. Although Guiteau never attained the fortune he so craved, he did, if only briefly, achieve the fame.

The Nineteenth Century Comes to a Close

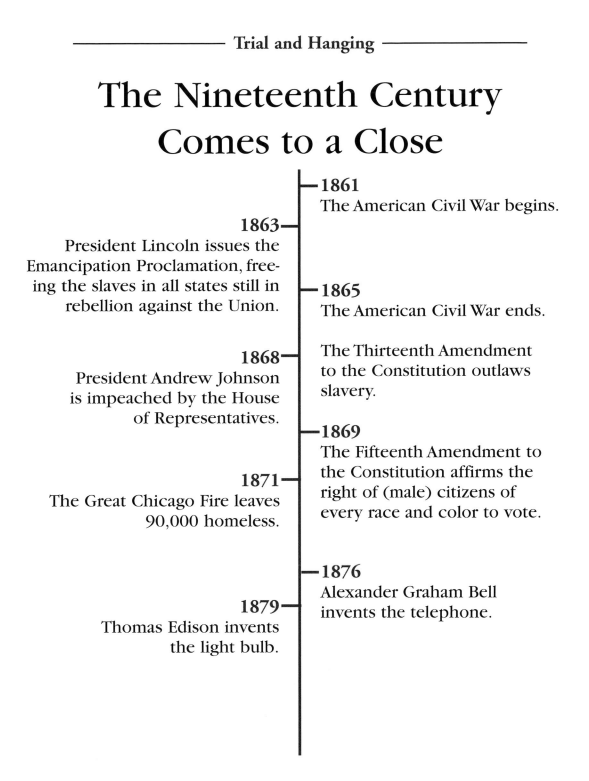

1861
The American Civil War begins.

1863
President Lincoln issues the Emancipation Proclamation, freeing the slaves in all states still in rebellion against the Union.

1865
The American Civil War ends.

The Thirteenth Amendment to the Constitution outlaws slavery.

1868
President Andrew Johnson is impeached by the House of Representatives.

1869
The Fifteenth Amendment to the Constitution affirms the right of (male) citizens of every race and color to vote.

1871
The Great Chicago Fire leaves 90,000 homeless.

1876
Alexander Graham Bell invents the telephone.

1879
Thomas Edison invents the light bulb.

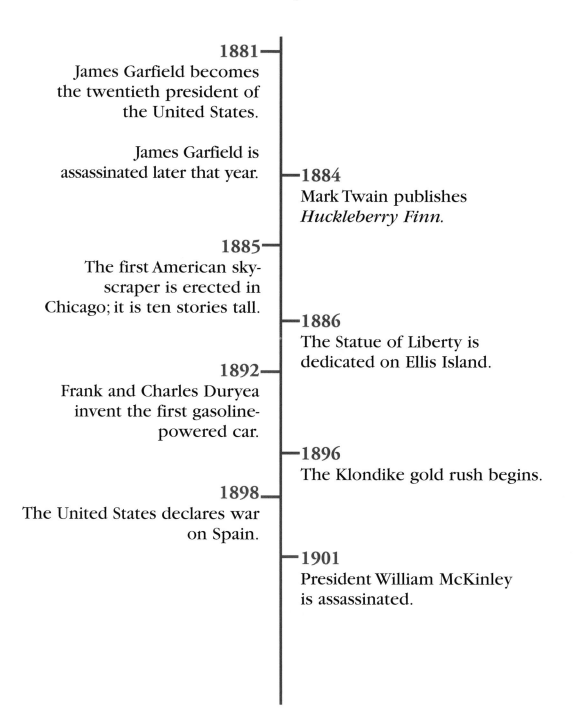

1881
James Garfield becomes the twentieth president of the United States.

James Garfield is assassinated later that year.

1884
Mark Twain publishes *Huckleberry Finn.*

1885
The first American skyscraper is erected in Chicago; it is ten stories tall.

1886
The Statue of Liberty is dedicated on Ellis Island.

1892
Frank and Charles Duryea invent the first gasoline-powered car.

1896
The Klondike gold rush begins.

1898
The United States declares war on Spain.

1901
President William McKinley is assassinated.

Glossary

abolish   To put an end to; to do away with.

ambitious   Having a strong desire to achieve a particular goal.

aneurysm   Enlargement or swelling of a part of an artery (or the heart), usually caused by a weakening of the artery's wall.

anticipate   To look forward to; to expect.

artery   Blood vessel that carries blood from the heart to any part of the body.

asylum   Place where the mentally ill are cared for.

autopsy   Examination of a body after death to determine the cause of death.

clemency   Act of showing mercy, leniency, or forgiveness toward someone who is to be punished.

colleague   Coworker or associate.

consul   Official appointed by a government to reside in a foreign country as a national representative.

destined   Chosen (as if by fate) to be or do something.

eloquence   Art or practice of speaking beautifully, powerfully, and convincingly.

evangelist   Preacher.

gallows   Upright, wooden frame used to hang criminals.

homeopathic   True to the principles of homeopathy, which is a method of treating disease using drugs in small doses that produce symptoms similar to those of the disease.

hyperactive   Unusually or abnormally active or energetic.

instinct   Natural impulse or reaction.

jurisdiction   Range of authority, power, or control of a judge or court.

malpractice   Failure of a professional, such as a doctor, to perform his duties properly because of a lack of knowledge or incompetence, especially when it leads to injury or death.

nuisance   Annoying or bothersome person or thing.

patriotism   Strong love, support, and defense of one's country.

preparatory school   Private school, often a boarding school, where the coursework is designed to prepare its students for college.

spectator   Person who looks on or watches.

Stalwart   Conservative Republican in the 1870s and 1880s, especially one who opposed the reform of the civil service.

stern   Having a definite hardness of nature.

For More Information

Charles Guiteau Collection
Georgetown University Lauinger Library
Special Collections Division: Archives, Manuscripts,
  Rare Books and Fine Prints
P.O. Box 571174
Washington, DC 20057-1174
(202) 687-7444
Web site: http://www.library-georgetown.edu/
  dept/specoll

James A. Garfield Birthplace
4350 S.O.M. Center Road
Moreland Hills
Cuyahoga County, OH 44022

James A. Garfield Collection
Williams College Library
Archives and Special Collections
55 Sawyer Library Drive
Williamstown, MA 01267
(413) 597-2501
Web site: http://www.williams.edu/library/archives

James A. Garfield National Historic Site
8095 Mentor Avenue
Mentor, OH 44060
(440) 255-8722
Web site: http://www.nps.gov/jaga

Web Sites

The American President
http://www.americanpresident.org/KoTrain/
    Courses/JG/JG_In_Brief.htm

**The Internet Public Library: Presidents of the
    United States**
http://www.ipl.org/ref/POTUS/jagarfield.html

The White House
http://www.whitehouse.gov/history/presidents/
    jg20.html

For Further Reading

Geary, Rick. *The Fatal Bullet: The True Account of the Assassination, Lingering Pain, Death, and Burial of President James A. Garfield, Twentieth President of the United States.* New York: Nantier-Beall-Minoustchine Publishing, Inc., 1999.

St. George, Judith. *In the Line of Fire: Presidents' Lives at Stake.* New York: Holiday House, 1999.

For Advanced Readers

Clark, James C. *The Murder of James A. Garfield: The President's Last Days and the Trial and Execution of His Assassin.* Jefferson, NC: McFarland & Company, Inc., 1993.

Leech, Margaret, and Harry J. Brown. *The Garfield Orbit.* New York: Harper & Row, 1978.

Lindop, Edmund. *Assassinations That Shook America.* New York: Franklin Watts, 1992.

Peskin, Allan. *Garfield: A Biography.* Kent, OH: Kent State University Press, 1999.

Index

About the Author

Robert Kingsbury lives in Philadelphia, Pennsylvania, with his wonderful wife and two darling daughters.

Photo Credits

Cover and pp. 8, 11, 17, 32, 36, 41, 43 © Bettmann/Corbis; pp. 1, 4, 10, 25, 34, 45, © Library of Congress, Prints & Photographs Division; pp. 9, 14, 18, 20, 31, 44, 49, 51, 53 © Culver Pictures Inc.; pp. 12, 26 © Hulton/Archive; pp. 29, 39, 46 reproduced from *The Life of Guiteau and the Official History of the Trial of Guiteau*.

Series Design and Layout

Les Kanturek

ƆUE